Dirty and clean fleece

Natural and dyed skeins

Natural cloth

Dyed cloth

A warp that has been tied and dyed

Cloth made from random-dyed threads

Cloth dyed after weaving

Preparation for dyeing

If fleece is going to be dyed before it is spun it should be thoroughly cleaned to remove all grease and dirt. (This is known as scouring).

1 Steeping

Place the well-opened-out fleece in clean hot water (50–55°C, 120–130°F). Allow the steeping to continue until the water is cold.

2 Scouring

Prepare a bowl of hot soapy water by using soap or your favourite synthetic detergent for wool. The water should feel hot to the hand (about 50–55°C, 120–130°F).

Immerse the fleece and *squeeze* it while it is in the liquid. Dirt and grease will quickly come out, but one wash will probably not be enough.

3 Rinsing

Rinse thoroughly in luke-warm water.

The fleece

Steep the fleece in clean hot water

Squeeze the dirty water out of the fleece gently

Skeining

When dyeing *yarn* it is worth taking trouble over making and tying skeins. If the threads get into a tangle a great deal of time will be wasted in trying to wind them into a ball or on a spool.

Check that the beginning and end are tied securely.

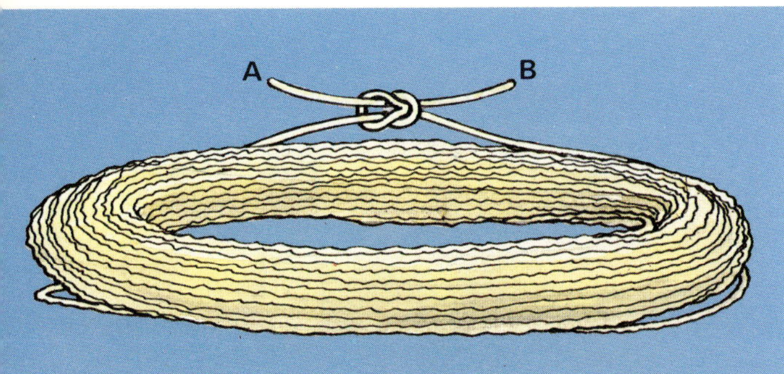

Another thread is then tied to ends A and B and tied loosely round the skein.

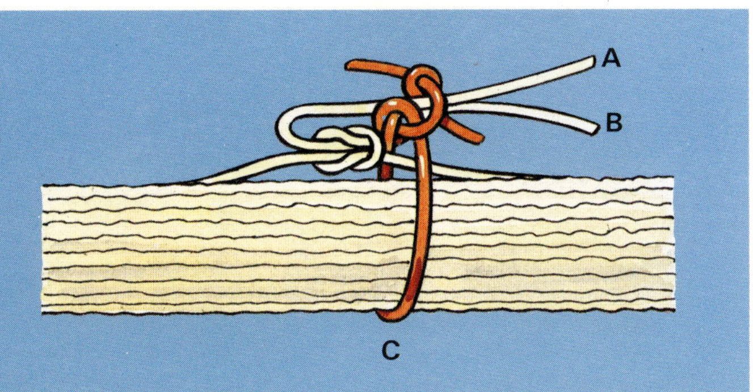

After checking the beginning and end of the skein, it should then be tied loosely in at least 2 places. This helps to keep the threads in order while they are being washed, stirred, dyed, rinsed and dried.

Use an undyed thread of a different thickness or texture so that it can easily be identified when it needs to be removed.

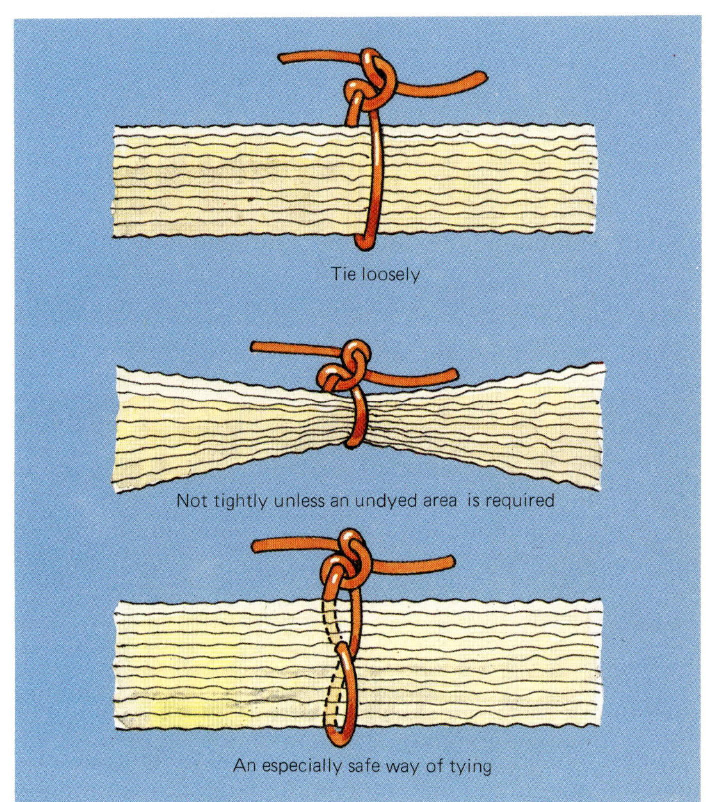

Dyeing

Most natural dyestuffs have to be boiled in a solution of one of several mineral salts (mordants), in order to make the colour fast, but beginners could start with two natural dyes which do not require that treatment.

Green walnuts

Collect green walnuts which fall off the tree in July and August.

Cover them with water and keep from the light.

Let them steep overnight and then simmer them in this water. Before immersing the thoroughly wetted wool strain off the walnuts.

If several skeins are placed in the dye-bath at first it will be possible to get various depths of colour by removing skeins at half hourly intervals.

Colours obtained from Green Walnut Husks

Lichen

Another useful dye, which does not need additional chemicals is *lichen*. If lichen is prolific in your area, collect some from rocks and trees. There are many varieties of lichen and they can produce rich colours.

When Parmelia saxatalis is boiled with the yarn or fabric it gives shades of brown and imparts a lovely aroma to the wool. This scent is associated with Harris tweed from the days when lichen was one of the dyes used.

Lichen swells in the rain, so it is easier to collect in damp weather.

Lichen

Colours obtained from Lichen

Method

Pack alternate layers of lichen and wool in the dye-bath, cover with soft water and simmer for 3 hours. Remove the wool from dye-bath, rinse and dry away from direct sunlight.

Mordants

Most natural dyes require a mordant to make them fast. The most commonly used mordants are:

ALUM – potassium aluminium sulphate
CHROME – potassium dichromate
IRON – ferrous sulphate
TIN – stannous chloride

Mordanting is an extremely important part of dyeing. It is worth carrying out this process with great care. SUCCESSFUL DYEING DEPENDS ON ACCURATE MORDANTING.

Containers of Alum, Chrome, Iron and Tin Mordants

Colours obtained from Elderberry

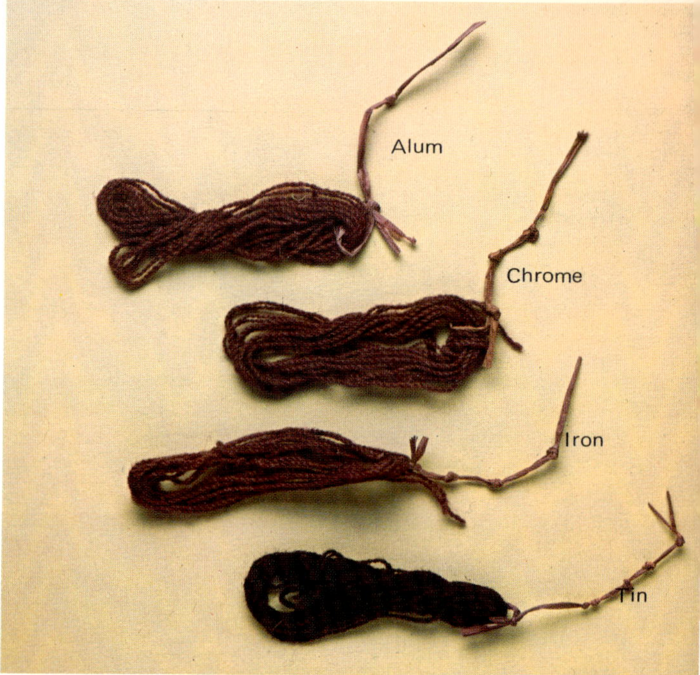

Mordants are used for 2 reasons:

1 To make the colour fast.
2 To change the shade.

In order to identify the mordants used it is helpful to devise a system of knots.

Use strong, undyed yarn, raffia, tape or string, and attach to the fleece, skein, etc. which is going to be mordanted.

One knot for ALUM, two knots for CHROME, three knots for IRON and four knots for TIN.

Method for using alum

USE 125g ALUM TO 500g WOOL (1 oz to 1 lb)

1 Mix alum with a little boiling water and add to the rest of the water in the bath.

2 When the water is about hand-heat enter the clean, thoroughly wetted wool.

3 Slowly bring the bath to almost boiling point and then simmer the wool for about an hour. Stir gently occasionally.

4 Remove the wool with a rod and let it drip over the bath for a few moments.

5 Gently squeeze out excess water.

The wool can be dyed at once, kept damp in a bag till next day or dried, stored and labelled for future use.

Alum is a very safe mordant to use, but be careful to use the right amount as too much alum will make the wool sticky.

Method for using chrome, iron and tin

These three mordants must be weighed extremely carefully because only a small amount is required.

USE 8g MORDANT TO 500g WOOL ($\frac{1}{4}$ oz to 1 lb)

Proceed as for alum, but after mordanting the wool different steps have to be taken.

1 **Chrome** is sensitive to light, so keep the wool covered and dye at once. Do not rinse before dyeing.

2 **Iron** is a difficult mordant to use, it can make dyes

The effect of four mordants on Stinging Nettle dye

uneven and can make the wool feel hard. Iron is often used **after** dyeing; this is known as a saddening process. The colours are dulled. Rinse thoroughly before dyeing.

3 **Tin** Mordanted wool should be washed in warm soapy water and rinsed in warm water before dyeing.

Cream of tartar is often used in conjunction with alum or iron mordant, to achieve a brighter and more even colour. It is added to the dyebath with the mordant at the rate of 30g to each 500g of wool (1 oz to 1 lb).

Dyeing with onion skins

To produce 4 different shades from one dye-bath.

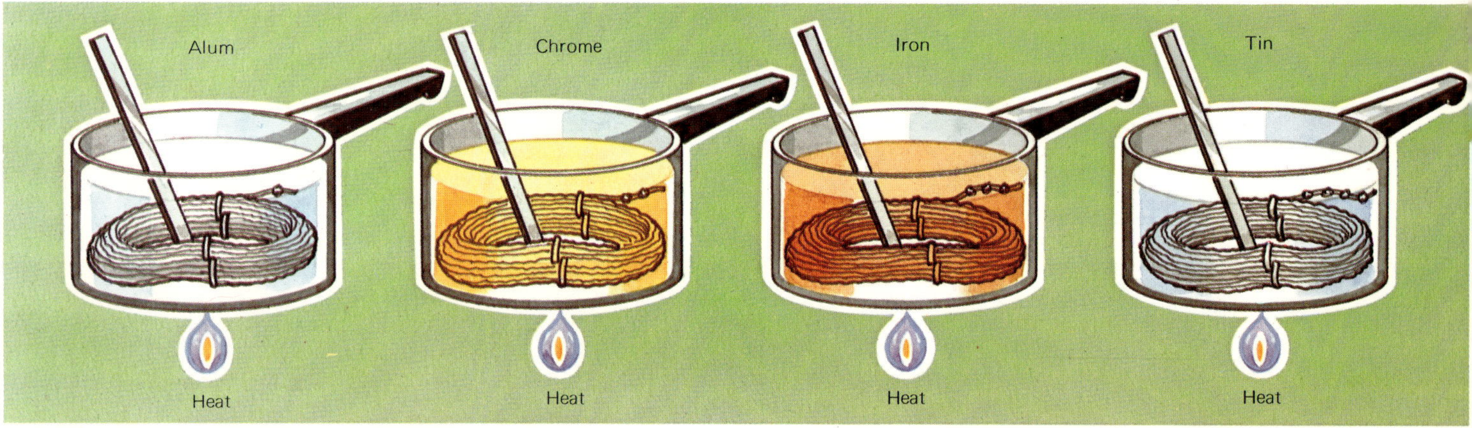

Mordanting the clean wet wool

4 skeins of clean wet wool weighing approximately 25 g each have been placed into the mordants.

While the wool is in the mordant prepare the dye-bath. Put about 0·125kg of onion skins into a pan of soft water; simmer for $\frac{1}{2}$ to 1 hour.

Strain off the skins, return liquor to dye-bath and when it has cooled to hand-heat it will be ready for the skeins of mordanted wool.

Remember to wash the skeins which have been mordanted in tin and iron, before lowering them into the dye-bath.

Slowly bring the bath to simmer, and simmer gently for at least 15 minutes. The colour deepens if the wool is left in the dye-bath longer.

Liquor obtained from onion skins

Dyeing with onion skins

When the colour looks dark enough remove the skeins with a rod, holding them over the dyebath for a few moments to allow them to drip. Rinse thoroughly and hang up to dry. Avoid bright sunlight.

Looking into the dyebath and seeing four shades of colour

Dyeing with onion skins

Keeping records

A record book and tie-on labels are useful.
Recipes can be written out and numbered so that the tie-on
label can quickly be fixed to the skein.

Information to be recorded:
Name of plant and part
The date
Time cooked
The mordant used

On one side the dried plant in a plastic bag with a sketch or
photograph underneath of its habitat. On the other side
samples and recipes.

Samples of every dyeing should be kept, with all information
necessary to repeat them. We cannot get exactly the same
colour next time, but it will be similar.
Do not throw away an unsuccessful pattern; record it, for it
might be just what is wanted another time.

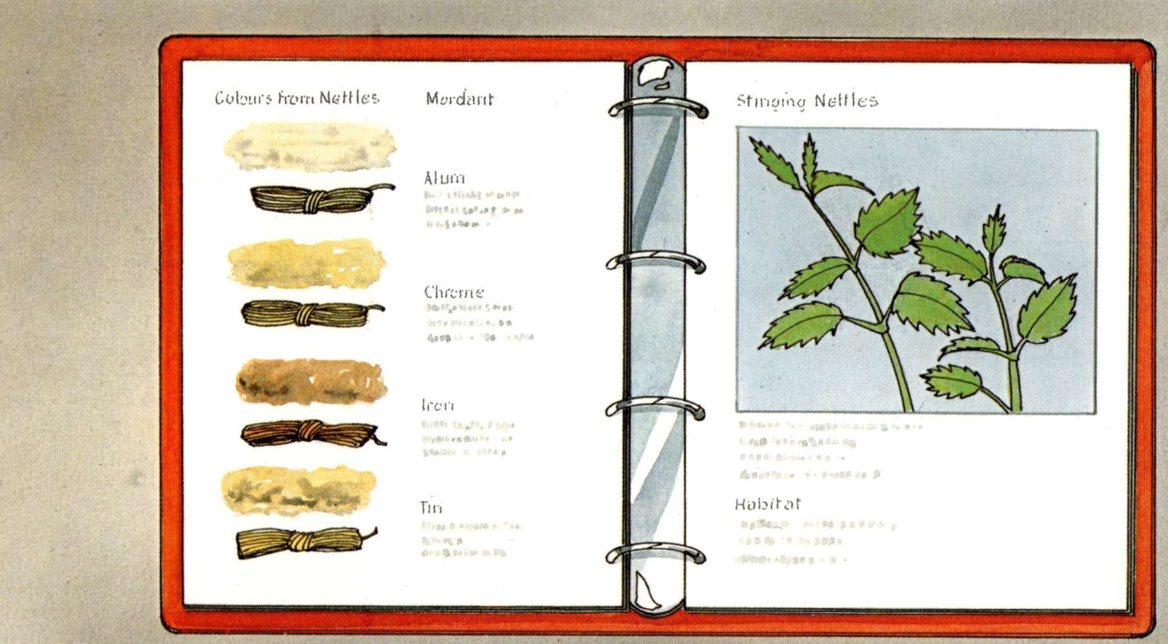

Sample record pages

A page from a record book

Sample: clear lemon yellow on wool.
Dyestuff: Wild mignonette (Reseda lutea) (Weld) from College garden July 1977.

Quantities:

Yarn: Handspun Welsh	0·125kg
Mordant: Alum	25 g
Dyestuff: dried	0·125kg
Water for each process	3·4 litres

Method

Mordanting. Well-wetted clean yarn put in mordant liquor 30°C. Raised to 100°C during 1 hour. Simmered at 95°C for 1 hour. Dyed immediately.

Dyeing. Chopped dyestuff boiled in enough water to cover for 2 hours. 3·4 litres of this liquid used for dyeing. Yarn entered at 30°C. Raised to boil during $\frac{1}{4}$ hour. Temperature maintained at 98°C for 1 hour. Yarn cooled, rinsed and dried.

Random dyed yarn

There are many ways in which skeins can be dyed in a variety of shades and colours.

Light to dark in one skein

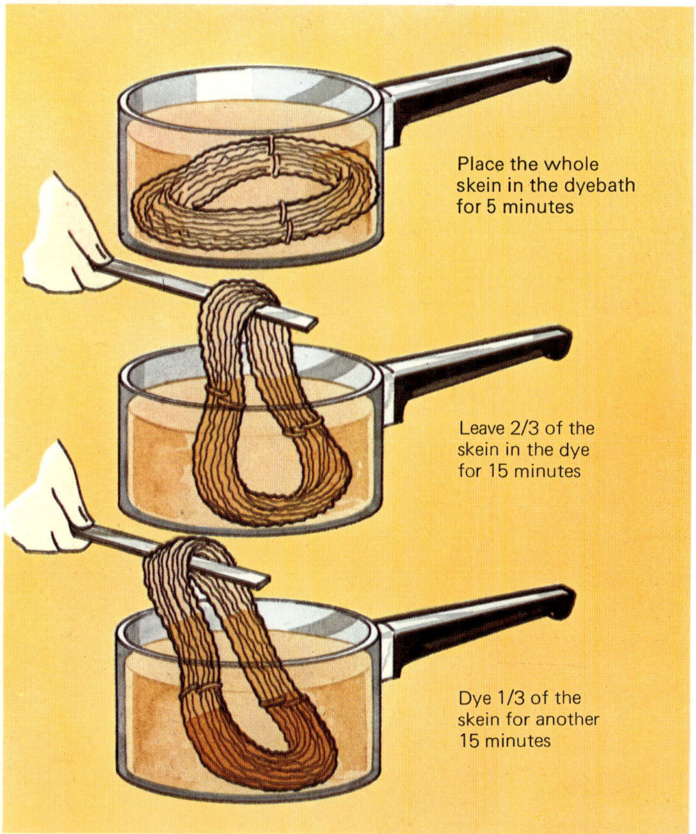

One mordant with 3 dyes

Make a fairly long skein and tie in the usual way. Prepare 3 dye-baths.

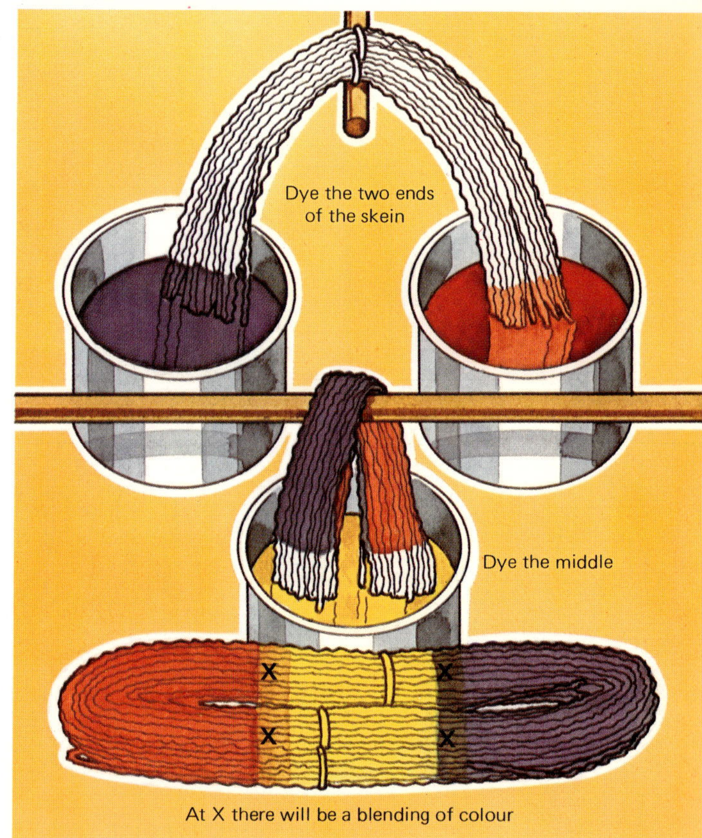